- Successful Dating -

No More Frogs
Capricorn

22 December – 19 January

by
Cathrine Dahl

CONTENTS

- Successful Dating -
No More Frogs

by Cathrine Dahl

No More Frogs - Successful Dating is your one-stop dating guide. No unnecessary blah-blah. The information is right here, at your fingertips.

This guide can be used in several ways. It's a handy tool when you want to prepare yourself a little. It can give you an advantage when going on a date or getting to know someone you've just met - or even someone you've known for a while.

Although this guide can help you angle your approach, remember to be true to yourself. Have fun, be wise, follow your heart - and keep your feet on the ground!

- Cathrine Dahl

Preface:
A few words about compatibility, and why compatibility guides can give you the wrong idea.

So you've met this Gemini you really, really like, but you're a Scorpio, and the compatibility guides say you're a lousy match. Guess what? That's rubbish!

Some compatibility guides offer a very simplistic approach, claiming that your best matches are the star signs within the same element as you:

Fire: Aries, Leo and Sagittarius
Earth: Taurus, Virgo and Capricorn
Air: Gemini, Libra and Aquarius
Water: Cancer, Scorpio and Pisces

Other guides are slightly more specific, declaring that we are compatible with star signs within our astrological polarity.

Yin: Taurus, Virgo, Capricorn, Cancer, Scorpio and Pisces
Yang: Aries, Leo, Sagittarius, Gemini, Libra and Aquarius

Doesn't look too good, does it? The most optimistic approach has removed half of the population from your dating pool. It doesn't make any sense. The true picture is far more promising...

One star sign, two very different personalities

Each of us has a unique astrological thumbprint determined by the sun, the moon and the planets. The most important factors being your ascending star (ascendant), the sun (star sign) and the moon (feelings).

Let's make it simple

Imagine your star sign being a melody. All the other aspects (the unique positioning of the moon and the planets) are sound effects, applied by a producer with a mixer.

The combination of rhythm, depth and base creates your unique sound. Another person with the same star sign will get his own sound mix and end up with a different beat.

Your personal melody can create wonderful harmonies with star signs you're not supposed to get on with – and nothing but noise with signs that are meant to be matches. You won't find out until you get to know each other.

Let's get to know your date...

THE MALE

YOUR DATE: CAPRICORN
22 December–19 January

The Essence of him

Ambitious – outgoing – friendly – persistent – extremely goal oriented – perseverant – believes in hard work without shortcuts – diplomatic – fair and just – cuts through details and gets to the chore – objective and down-to-earth – good with money – loves luxury and quality – carefully optimistic – an excellent host and entertaining guest – loyal – reliable – dependable – intelligent

...and remember: This man will always reach his goals – if he puts his mind to it. Don't rush him. He needs to figure things out and move ahead at his own pace.

Blind Date – speedy essentials

Who's waiting for you?

You probably won't notice him right away: the classily dressed man standing towards the side of the room. He is glancing at everyone who comes through the door without being obvious about it or drawing attention to himself. This man is a master when it comes to observing. If you decided to have a few drinks before meeting him and enter the restaurant slightly tipsy and with your outfit messed up, he'll probably turn around and ignore you. This guy will not go out with a woman who doesn't meet his standards.

Emergency fixes for embarrassing pauses

Even though he may come across as masculine and outgoing, he will expect you to play an active part in the conversation – not only because he wants to check you out, but also because men born under this sign can be a little shy at times. If the conversation feels a little slow, take the initiative to talk about topics you know something about. He will appreciate a woman with her own opinions.

Your place or mine?

Sex on the first date? Very unlikely. Sex is something he saves – usually – until he has captured a woman he is romantically interested in. However, there are exceptions. He may want to join you at your place if he's afraid of losing the chance of getting to know you further. But if you really like him, it's better to save the erotic invitations until later. A little patience now can bring you loads of passion later.

Checklist, before you dash out to meet him:
Don't be late
(hint: Avoid keeping him waiting)
Look stylish from head to toe
(hint: No cheap imitations)
Don't pre-drink with girlfriends
(hint: Giggly and slightly tipsy is a no-no)
Brush up on a few topics you're interested in
(hint: He appreciates a smart woman)
Check out some places you could go
(hint: A cool bar or even a special exhibition)

Tip: Don't get too creative. This is a cool, conservative and determined man. Go for classy rather than sassy, both when it comes to appearance and approach.

CHAPTER 1

PREPARE YOURSELF

Catch his eye, capture his attention
Top 10 attention grabbers

1. Be classy. No flashy outfits.
2. Carry yourself with poise – and keep a playful sparkle in your eyes.
3. Show interest in what he's doing and what he has done before.
4. Be open and genuine in your approach.
5. Ask questions, and be smart about it.
6. Admire him, but only if it's called for and he deserves it. No fake compliments!
7. Be cheerful, optimistic and outgoing.
8. Show him that you have an independent mind and your own opinions.
9. Be flexible in your views, but don't compromise your own opinions.
10. Let him know that you appreciate a man being a man.

The SHE. The woman!

The Capricorn male regards himself as a true man, in the traditional sense of the word: strong, reliable and masculine. His partner must be able to appreciate these qualities in order to enjoy him. His perfect woman does not compete with him, but rather makes the picture complete. She is independent and intelligent, but never aggressive or pushy. She is feminine, but never girly and giggly. She is cool, classy – and his feminine reflection.

The Essence of her

Feminine – intelligent – cheerful – attractive – appreciates masculinity and the strength of a man – well-mannered – enjoys chivalrous attention – carries herself like a woman – independent – supportive – loyal – optimistic – encouraging when days are grey – shows respect and admiration for her partner's efforts, both at work and in their personal life – applauds his ambition

Capricorn arousal meter

From 0 to 100... One hour – or one year! The Capricorn man is extremely patient, and he can hold back until he has captured his woman...

Remember: Be true to yourself

It doesn't matter if he is the most stunning guy you've ever met – if you don't match, you don't match. You may be able to put on a show for a while to hold his attention, but what's the point? We can't please everybody. We all have different needs, dreams, tastes and preferences. There's no such thing as a one-size-fits-all lover. Be yourself, and be true to who you are – always!

Very important: Don't be too fixed in your ways. Flexibility is the key to getting on with this guy. When he's stubborn, go for a diplomatic approach.

CHAPTER 2

THE FIRST DATE

Getting your foot in the door
The basics

Femininity rules. Your attitude is very important. If you find it difficult to live out your feminine side and allow a man to be a man, you may have a problem.

Be attentive. As soon as you've got his attention, be attentive, listen and ask questions.

Genuine admiration. Feel free to admire him and pay him compliments, but only do so genuinely. Never feign positive attention with this guy.

Trigger his curiosity. There must be something about you that sparks his interest – something that isn't too obvious. This could be a discreet, playful glance, perhaps, or a feminine outfit ... anything that triggers his subconscious desire.

Stand on your own feet. Being smart and independent is always a great plus – provided there is still plenty of room for a masculine male in your life.

Grace and flexibility. He appreciates an easygoing woman who knows how to carry herself. Rigid women drive him nuts.

Whatever you do...

• **DON'T** interrupt him or disagree loudly.

• **DON'T** use crude language.

• **DON'T** express a negative outlook on life.

• **DON'T** be hyper-positive and out-of-touch with reality.

• **DON'T** pretend to know more about a topic than you

do.

Remember,

There are no shortcuts to his heart. Even if he is interested in you, feelings need to

- **DON'T** wear anything eye-popping, even if it's

fashionable.

- **DON'T** serve him white lies in order to impress him.

- **DON'T** be sexually aggressive.

- **DON'T** criticize him when he's being gallant.

- **DON'T** forget your manners. Mind what you say and do.

develop naturally. Don't push him. Be patient.

Signs you're in - or not

Love at first sight is not really the Capricorn man's thing. He is far too analytical to allow himself to get carried away by feelings that haven't had a chance to develop naturally. However, he will observe you closely, and if he feels the two of you may have more potential than a nice evening, he will pursue you. If you have made a thorough impression on him, he will probably be quite persistent in his approach. When he's on to something good, there's only one option: success. The following are some clear indications that he's got his eyes on you:

Chances are he will...

- call or text you the next day
- suggest going out very soon after your first date
- pamper you in an old-fashioned way: flowers, dinner, etc.
- be attentive and help you with personal or professional tasks
- share his personal views and ideas with you
- act protective when you are around other guys

Not your type? Making an exit

The Capricorn man is practical in all areas of life, including his love life. If things are not working out, he'll talk to you about it and try to figure something out. If there's nothing more to build on, he will suggest moving on. Being stuck in a relationship is not his thing. He needs to have a purpose in everything he does. Everything must be growing and moving

moving forward. Love is a living thing. If it's withering, he will find more nourishing soil.

However, there are Capricorns who refuse to see what's going on and who insist on making it work, because if you put your mind to it, it will ... right? These men need to be kicked out of their comfort zone. Forcing them to touch base with reality can actually help them move forward and thrive.

Foolproof exit measures:

These strategies will make you look like an idiot. But if that's what it takes to send him out of your life, well ... that's what it takes!

- Be crude in language and appearance
- Insist that he spend more time with you than on his interests
- Tell silly jokes in bed and give the impression that sex is purely a physical thing
- Start throwing your money around
- Criticize him for being polite and attentive, saying that this isn't the 1950s
- Pick arguments whenever you can and disagree loudly

CHAPTER 3

SEX'N STUFF

Seductive moves:
How to get him in the mood:

It is your mind, not the size of your bra, that will spark his erotic interest. Combine your alert mind with closeness and intimacy, and he will start to ease into sensual feelings. A seductive glance can do more for him than any other man in the zodiac. Add a bit of slow, seductive dancing and he'll be ready to go.

Preferences and erotic nature

The Capricorn man will always make an effort, and he expects his woman to do the same. In order to make him happy, you should always pay close attention to what he enjoys in bed. Remember the details, and introduce them next time you have sex with him. He can go all night without tiring, and he has a unique ability to satisfy his partner. Forget acrobatic stunts: he believes in the quiet and intense pleasures of sex and prefers them in comfortable surroundings – not in the backseat of a car! No matter how much you try to persuade him, this man won't let his trousers drop until he feels comfortable. Never, ever try to tell him what to do. He's got firm opinions about sex and won't allow himself to be pushed into something he's not comfortable with.

Hitting the right buttons

Although every sign has areas on the body that are more sensitive than others, individual sensitivity may vary quite a bit. Don't go body-blind. Honing in on these erogenous zones and forgetting the rest of him is not a good idea. Use these areas to create sparks while turning him on, and as a passion-booster when things get heated. Watch his body language – including the most obvious of signs. Open your mind to the sensuality of touch and taste.

Key areas
The entire back

Get it on
If he asks you to give him a backrub, be careful and aware of what you are doing, because his erogenous zone is his back! If you're not in the mood for sex, you need to make sure the massage resembles a rough physiotherapy treatment.

Arouse him
On the other hand, if you want to experience the erotic side of him, be gentle with your massage – very gentle. Apply oil or cream to facilitate smooth movement over his back. Let your hands brush over his buttocks, lower back and sides, but be careful not to tickle him. What may put other guys to sleep will have the opposite effect on him.

Surprise him

Put on some slow music and start unbuttoning his shirt while the two of you are dancing. This should spark his interest. Continue dancing on your own while slowly stripping all your clothes off.

Spice it up

Take the backrub a bit further. Gently apply some whipped cream or sweet liqueur to his back and playfully lick it off.

Remember: Although he is a strong and confident lover, he relies heavily on feedback from his partner during sex. Let him know how you feel.

His expectations

No erotic expeditions. His ideal woman mustn't be too demanding or adventurous. If sex is turned into some kind of erotic expedition with little closeness or sensitivity, he'll lose interest.

Be present, be active. She must be feminine, tender and actively participating. A date who leaves everything to him won't get a second chance. In fact, he can be offended by a passive partner.

No cheeky stuff. The atmosphere needs to be right, and the surroundings comfortable. Don't suggest a quick one in an unusual place. This is not his thing.

Sensual guidance. He doesn't expect his partner to be an erotic expert. He is more than willing to teach, inspire and guide an inexperienced woman, which can be a great boost to the relationship.

Nourish his masculinity. He enjoys a woman who truly appreciates his masculinity. The appreciation will make him even more eager to please her.

Time and place. If he's not in the mood, he's not in the mood! If he's got too much going on in his mind, he won't be able to free his body and relax.

Your sensual preferences
Quiz yourself and find out whether this man is for you.

Where on the scale are you?
1 = Don't agree | 3 = Sure | 5 = Agree!

1. Comfortable and private surroundings are important for enjoying sex.
One a scale for 1 to 5, you are: 1 - 2 - 3- 4 - 5

2. Erotic acrobatics are distracting and diminish pleasure.
One a scale for 1 to 5, you are: 1 - 2 - 3- 4 - 5

3. Intimacy and chemistry do more for passion than sex toys.
One a scale for 1 to 5, you are: 1 - 2 - 3- 4 - 5

4. Atmosphere is very important for creating a sensual mood.
One a scale for 1 to 5, you are: 1 - 2 - 3- 4 - 5

Score 15–20: The two of you are incredibly attuned to each other. There will be a lot of pleasure ahead.
Score 10–14: Sex with him might be a little slower and more intense than what you're used to, but the pleasure and satisfaction will probably be amazing.
Score 5–9: It's very important to communicate – otherwise, the two of you might lose out on significant pleasure. Get to know each other's preferences. Don't be afraid to ask.
Score 1–4: You may be a little too restless to enjoy this man as a lover. Slowing down could broaden your horizons. Try it.

CHAPTER 4

GENERAL STUFF

The big picture

Keep in mind that the characteristics of a Capricorn may vary quite a bit depending on where within the sign he was born, as well as a wide range of additional astrological factors. But for now, let's stick to the basics. Just remember: don't jump to conclusions as soon as you meet him. Give him room to shine. Get to know the man behind the sign.

His personality: Pros and cons

Pros	Cons
• Attentive	• Chauvinistic
• Charming	• Traditional
• Thorough	• Conservative
• Persistent	• A slow mover
• Loyal	• A lone wolf
• Confident and friendly	• Snobbish
• Grounded and controlled	• Stubborn
• Optimistic	• Self-centred
• A born leader	• Fixed in his views
• Trustworthy	• Critical
• Classy and stylish	• Inflexible
• Intelligent	• Controlling
• Patient	• Judgmental
• An excellent host	• Has high expectations

Tip: How to show romantic interest

Show genuine admiration for him. Be supportive of his ideas. Do something that shows our effort, like making him his dinner or suggesting an activity based on something you know he's interested in.

Romantic Vibes

Mr Capricorn:
The strong and chivalrous partner

The essence

A lone rider. He may come across as a guy who can move through life perfectly well on his own – and he probably could. However, he prefers to have a woman by his side.

True love. His partner needs to provide love, support and inspiration; she will give him the affirmation he needs.

No time wasters, please. He doesn't throw his love around and is prepared to take his time searching for the woman of his dreams.

Loving actions. He sometimes finds it difficult to express his feelings with words, and his partner needs to know how to interpret actions that signal his love.

Enjoy time together. He is attentive, loving and caring. It's not his style to spend the evenings out on the town with his friends. When he has found a woman he truly cares about, he will want to spend time with her.

...but pursue interests separately. It's important to him to be able to pursue hobbies and interests individually. This can enrich the relationship and make the bond stronger.

No quitter. He will never leave at the first sight of friction. He will stay and try his best to work things out.

Tip: How to show erotic interest

Get closer to him physically, without being obvious about it. Establish closeness when you're out walking or dancing. But be careful not to come across as clingy – that will turn him off.

Erotic Vibrations

Mr Capricorn:
The intense and determined lover

The essence

No demanding sexual athlete. He doesn't seek erotic fulfillment whenever possible. The interest is there, but it's seldom imposing.

Quiet beauty of sex. He's not into erotic acrobatics or wild nights. This guy prefers the quiet beauty of sex: closeness, intimacy and tenderness. But this doesn't mean he's not passionate. He is sensual, highly erotic and difficult to resist.

Mindful sensuality. For him, sex is seldom about pure physical satisfaction. The emotional side is just as important.

Sensual emotions. Words of love don't come naturally to him, and he often prefers to show his feelings during sex. This can make the sensual moments very intense and tender.

Erotic thermostat. He needs to let the erotic temperature develop naturally.

Stamina. He's not the most sexually creative guy in the zodiac, but he makes up for it with intensity and endurance.

Brings out the best in her. He has a unique ability to make his woman feel like a naughty princess in bed, regardless of how much experience she may or may not have.

CHAPTER 5

COMPATIBILITY QUIZ

Are you banging your head against the wall, or does he unleash your positive potential? Do you provoke him or bring out the best in him? Does he make you throw your arms up in exasperation, or do you feel inspired and complete in his company? Are the two of you headed towards doom or dream? Take the test to find out.

Question 1.
Is it important to you that your partner express his feelings with words?

A. I'm not particular about how he does it, as long as he manages to his feelings in one way or another.
B. Of course. How else am I supposed to know how he feels?
C. Not really, but sometimes it's nice to hear sweet nothings.

Question 2.
What male personality do you find it easiest to connect with?

A. Someone who's playful and boyish.
B. A stylish and passionate guy.
C. A persistent and ambitious type.

(cont.)

Question 3.
Do you enjoy having sex in new and unusual places, or do you prefer comfortable surroundings?

A. I prefer comfortable and romantic settings.
B. Traditional lovemaking is not my style. I enjoy new experiences, including new places to have sex.
C. Although I've been dreaming about sex on the beach in the moonlight, I tend toward comfortable surroundings in real life.

Question 4.
Do you consider yourself goal-oriented and persistent?

A. Sometimes. It depends on how important the goal is to me.
B. Yes. Setting goals is the first step to success.
C. Not really. I don't have the patience.

Question 5.
Do you think it's important to express love during sex?

A. Yes, but it all depends on the mood. Sometimes I just want a bit of passion.
B. Yes, absolutely. It can elevate the pleasure to new heights.
C. Sex and love are two different things. Why try to mix them?

Question 6.
What does it take to get you in the mood?

A. An expensive gift.
B. A few tender words whispered into your ear.
C. A nice dinner at an intimate restaurant.

Question 7.
How would you feel if a nice guy showed interest in you – and was very persistent about it?

A. I'd love it. It would make me feel desired.
B. Annoyed. I can't stand pushy guys.
C. I don't know. It would depend on whether I really liked him or not.

Question 8.
Do you find it easy to adjust to new situations?

A. Usually it's no problem.
B. Not really. I'm pretty set in my ways.
C. It all depends. If I have met a really nice man, I can be pretty flexible.

Question 9.
Does material success mean a lot to you?

A. Not at all. There are many more important things in life.
B. Yes. It's a reward for working hard and striving towards your goals.
C. Yes, but I'm not completely fixated on it.

Question 10.
Do you mind if your man pursues interests on his own?

A. It's fine, provided he's not away every night or every weekend.
B. No. It's important to do things together. It will make the relationship more rewarding.
C. Yes! What's the point having a relationship if we're not doing things together?

SCORE	A	B	C
Question 1	10	1	5
Question 2	1	5	10
Question 3	10	1	5
Question 4	5	10	1
Question 5	5	10	1
Question 6	1	5	10
Question 7	10	1	5
Question 8	10	1	5
Question 9	1	10	5
Question 10	5	10	1

75 – 100

The two of you make a power duo in every aspect of life. You inspire and support each other. You communicate with minimal misunderstandings. You share love and affection on a unique level, and your feelings are expressed through everything you do – and no matter what you choose to do, you make a perfect team. This special relationship has the potential to grow and become stronger throughout life. You have managed to become friends, partners and lovers: a true recipe for happiness.

51 – 74

You probably know it already – but this feels good. You admire his drive and strength; he cherishes your enthusiasm, support and loyalty. You bring that extra spark to his life, and he makes sure your life is safe and comfortable. Sure, there will be a few lively discussions from time to time, but they will prevent the relationship from becoming boring. You share a mutual respect and are able to inspire each other. Sometimes you don't even have to say anything; the things you do will spark ideas and creativity. Enjoy!

26 – 50

Love is not always a walk in the park, and sometimes achieving happiness and fulfillment requires effort. You may find yourself debating quite a few things in this relationship. Even though you love him, certain elements of his personality drive you nuts from time to time, especially when he's being extremely focused and persistent. Sometimes you wish he'd be a little more playful and spontaneous, –not so serious about life all the time. He makes you feel safe and desired, but what about your happiness? You need to figure out what's important to you and whether he fits into your life. Keep in mind that a life worth having is worth fighting for – no matter if he's there or not.

10 – 25

If you don't leave, he probably will – and that says a lot, because this man is not a quitter. At this point, you need to figure out what you're doing: are you spending time together or wasting time together? If you don't have anything to offer each other besides irritation and negative vibes, it's time to move on. Don't let pride get in the way. Cutting through when things are not working is not a failure; it's constructive and productive. Both of you need to thrive, and the best way to do this is to define your values, follow your heart and move on.

Thoughts...

If you really want something. If you feel it's right. If you know it'll be difficult - but worth it... Go for it!

Sometimes, making an effort makes the reward much more satisfying.

THE FEMALE

YOUR DATE: CAPRICORN
22 December–19 January

The Essence of her

Stylish – feminine – persistent– independent, but longing for a strong and protective man by her side – ambitious – a passionate lover – perfectionistic – loyal and reliable – efficient – optimistic – snobbish – reserved before she gets to know someone – stubborn –intelligent – has an eye for beauty and quality in everything around her – hard-working

...and remember: Although she may come across as cool and reserved, she is warm, genuine and affectionate when you get to know her.

Blind Date – speedy essentials

Who's waiting for you?

She might be a little early, but she's usually right on time. If you're not there, she will start wondering if she got the time messed up. She's reluctant to think you're sloppy and not able to keep a date. In other words: don't be late! A Capricorn woman carries herself with an aura of grace and femininity. She may seem a little cool and reserved at first, but she'll lighten up as soon as she feels comfortable around you. There is something dignified about her, but if you look closely, you'll notice a cheeky glint in her eyes. She offers far more than what your first impression might trick you into believing.

Emergency fixes for embarrassing pauses.

She's far too polite to allow embarrassing pauses to occur. If the conversation slows down, she will take the initiative to talk about different topics. However, if this does happen, it probably means the two of you haven't hit it off, and she will probably make an excuse to leave early.

Your place or mine?

Neither. The Capricorn woman is not into casual sex or superficial flings. If you imply any erotic intent during your first date, you may push her away. But don't be fooled into thinking that she's not interested in sex, because she is. She can be very passionate and determined in bed. However, she needs to feel comfortable around her partner before she can fully appreciate the physical sensations.

Checklist, before you dash out to meet her:

Be polished and groomed

(hint: Be classy)

Carry small items of luxury, old or new: a watch, a pen, etc. (hint: Show good taste)

Make sure everything is organized: tickets, table and transport (hint: Pamper her)

Be up-to-date on the arts scene, or something similar (hint: Be interesting)

Have your wallet ready...

(hint: Don't be cheap)

Tip: She appreciates style, quality and a little luxury – but never confuse money with class. A thick gold chain nesting in a hairy chest is (usually) a big no-no!

CHAPTER 1

PREPARE YOURSELF

_____

Catch her eye, capture her attention
Top 10 attention grabbers

1. Be gallant and carry yourself with poise.
2. Show off subtle signs of luxury like nice shoes or a watch (but no flashy bling).
3. Offer your assistance if someone needs it.
4. Take the initiative to invite her out.
5. Be strong and independent, but still attentive and gentle.
6. Let her in on your ideas for the future, but also let her see that you have your feet on the ground.
7. Emphasise some of the things you are good at without bragging.
8. Ask for her opinion and compliment her ideas.
9. Namedropping is fine, provided it fits into the conversation naturally.
10. Maintain a warmth in your expression.

The HE. The man!

You've either got it or you don't. The Capricorn woman will discern very quickly whether you're the type of guy she's looking for. If she's not sure, she will probably give you a second chance. However, there are a few basic requirements. She loves having a man around that makes her feel like a woman. She doesn't mind a good-looking body, but she values intelligence, so you must be able to flex more than just your biceps.

The Essence of him
Stylish and classy – intelligent – well informed, especially about things she can apply to her life (like food, drink and the arts) – independent – ambitious – strong and protective, with a masculine attitude – passionate and sensual – attractive and well-groomed – optimistic – supportive – appreciative of the good things in life, but not prone to throw money around

---

Capricorn arousal meter
From 0 to 100... Fifteen minutes. There's a time and place for everything. If the setting is right, she will warm up to your erotic advances very quickly.

Remember: Be true to yourself

It doesn't matter if she is the most stunning girl you've ever met – if you don't match, you don't match. You may be able to put on a show for a while to hold her attention, but what's the point? We can't please everybody. We all have different needs, dreams, tastes and preferences. There's no such thing as a one-size-fits-all lover. Be yourself, and be true to who you are – always!

Very important: The Capricorn woman values quality in every area of life. Make sure you are genuine in everything you do. Be stylish. Be charming. Be strong.

CHAPTER 2

THE FIRST DATE

Getting your foot in the door
The basics

Don't get too personal. A casual 'Tell me about yourself' won't work. The Capricorn woman will not reveal her thoughts and feelings to someone she doesn't know.

Patience pays off. Her attitude can cause some men to regard her as out-of-reach, but that's not the case. It just takes a little patience.

No erotic advances. She is cool, controlled and not keen on casual sex – no matter how dishy the guy might be.

Smooth and classy. Be a gentleman. She's not attracted to showoffs or people who throw money around.

Be informed. Take a genuine interest in what goes on in the world. Read a couple of books or visit an art exhibition before seeing her – or at least check out reviews on the internet.

No showing off. Don't be superficial or pretend to know more about something than you do. She will call your bluff.

Give her a small gift, preferably a little luxury.

Whatever you do...

- **DON'T** come across as cheap. Treat her to something nice.

- **DON'T** brag about your job, your car or whatever.

- **DON'T** criticize independent women.

- **DON'T** be rude to the waiter or to people around you.

- **DON'T** forget your manners. Be polite and attentive.

Remember,
If she thinks she's been wrong about you, she will disappear quickly.

• **DON'T** ask her about personal or sensitive issues if

you've just met.

• **DON'T** start a discussion just for the sake of it.

• **DON'T** expect her to split the check.

• **DON'T** suggest having sex on the first date.

• **DON'T** be late or forget to call her the next day.

Never get too comfortable
and take her attention
for granted. Keep being
charming!

Signs you're in - or not

This woman will actually let you know that she likes you. She may not walk up to you and say 'Hey!', but she will make it clear through her attitude and her actions that you have captured her interest and eventually her heart. She is persistent in every area of her life, including romance and sensuality. She believes that anything worth having is worth fighting for, and if you have captured her heart – she will make an effort to keep you in her life. Although the signs are usually quite clear, you may also want to keep an eye out for the following:

Chances are she will...

- show up at a function that she knows you will be attending, looking stunning
- make an effort to dazzle you with her looks and femininity
- casually give you a small – but expensive! – gift
- offer to help you with something
- emphasise her admiration for you
- take the initiative to call and text you

Not your type? Making an exit

The Capricorn woman is patient, a true 'stayer'. If she feels that a man is worth the effort, she will wait, work and try to sort things out. She may even get quite stubborn about it. This stubbornness can result from a mixture of hurt feelings and hurt pride. Having to admit that she failed in a relationship – as well as having her heart crushed – can be too much to handle. In these situations, she will try to find reasons to stay, and she will try to convince her partner to stay as well.

If you're not interested in keeping the relationship going, and if you know that happiness waits for both of you elsewhere, you may have to be blunt. Don't give her any cause to misinterpret your actions. Be perfectly clear about what you're doing, and make her realise that choosing you was a mistake.

Foolproof exit measures:

Before you go ahead with any of these suggestions, be prepared to look like an idiot. She will probably get mad and tell you to get a grip before she dumps you.

- Give her a cheap gift that you picked up at a gas station
- Meet her for a date unshaven and wearing dirty clothes
- Forget to bring your wallet and make her pay for the date
- Get overly emotional about everything
- Tell her that you are thinking about giving up your job and becoming a poet
- Show little or no interest in sex – unless it's in a public restroom or in the backseat of your car

CHAPTER 3

SEX'N STUFF

Seductive moves:
How to get her in the mood:

This is actually quite easy. The Capricorn woman enjoys frequent sex and doesn't mind taking the lead. However, she will also appreciate the initiative coming from her man. She doesn't need long-lasting foreplay. The erotic sparks fly freely and quickly from her, and she is usually ready to enjoy her partner in no time.

Preferences and erotic nature

She is attracted to strong, cultivated, polite and stylish men. A man who manages to reveal a physical interest simply by looking at her will also make her heart beat faster. As soon as you have won her trust and affection, turning her on will be easy – she will actually expect you to. If you can show your affection through a seductive smile and a gentle kiss, she will probably respond in kind. A lazy partner will not remain in her life for long. She enjoys being erotically assertive and may start undressing you when she feels the mood coming on, and then it won't take long before she has seduced you completely...

Hitting the right buttons

Although every sign has areas on the body that are more sensitive than others, individual sensitivity may vary quite a bit. Don't go body-blind. Honing in on these erogenous zones and forgetting the rest of her is not a good idea. Use these areas to create sparks while turning her on, and as a passion-booster when things get heated. Watch her body language – including the most obvious of signs. Open your mind to the sensuality of touch and taste.

Key areas
Her back and stomach

Get it on
The Capricorn woman is sensual and erotic, a dream to turn on. Pay attention to her lower back, and you will get results very quickly. Light touches, soft kisses and even a gentle massage will make her tingle inside...

Arouse her
The possibilities for arousing her are almost endless. Two areas in particular that will respond extremely well to kisses and gentle nibbles are the tender skin around her navel and the backs of her knees. These can be described as magic spots. If she seems reluctant to have sex, a gentle flicker with your tongue in these areas may change all that.

Surprise her

Treat her to a private show. She enjoys undressing her partner, but this time, only allow her to watch. Be seductive, be erotic and tease her until she simply has to touch you.

Spice it up

Although she's not into elaborate foreplay, whipped cream or a touch of honey around her navel followed by a playful tongue can add a passionate dimension to make the sex even more intense.

Remember: Although she is passionate and erotic, she prefers to have sex in comfortable surroundings. Never suggest anywhere out of the ordinary.

Her expectations

Exploring the flavours of the main course. No need to worry if you're not a foreplay expert. She doesn't mind moving onto the real thing more or less right away.

Takes the initiative. She enjoys being assertive in bed and often initiates sex.

Stick to the menu. Don't introduce any erotic surprises while having sex. She prefers to know what to expect.

No erotic circus. Erotic gymnastics are not her style. She prefers the traditional pleasures of sex.

Sensual enthusiasm. She is passionate and enthusiastic, and she always manages to turn traditional positions into something new and exciting.

Bring out the passion. She expects passion and sensual enthusiasm from her partner.

Pace yourself. Never push her. She enjoys exploring sex at her own pace. If you really need her to move on, let her know gently.

Visual stimulus. Watching her partner undress slowly and seductively, can create sudden erotics sparks.

Your sensual preferences
Quiz yourself and find out whether this woman is for you.

Where on the scale are you?
1 = Don't agree | 3 = Sure | 5 = Agree!

1. Passion is very important for a fulfilling sex life.
One a scale for 1 to 5, you are: 1 - 2 - 3- 4 - 5

2. Frequent sex makes a relationship more energetic and inspiring.
One a scale for 1 to 5, you are: 1 - 2 - 3- 4 - 5

3. Being undressed or undressing someone else can be very arousing in itself.
One a scale for 1 to 5, you are: 1 - 2 - 3- 4 - 5

4. Sex can be fulfilling even without sex toys or new positions.
One a scale for 1 to 5, you are: 1 - 2 - 3- 4 - 5

Score.
15 - 20: You are passionate, erotic and well matched to her.
10 - 14: She may take you by surprise a couple of times, but her passion and assertiveness thrill you.
05 - 09: She may be a little too much for you at times, but other times, you wish she could be more adventurous. Communicate your needs.
01 - 04: Both of you may broaden your horizons if you listen and learn from each other.

CHAPTER 4

GENERAL STUFF

The big picture

Keep in mind that the characteristics of a Capricorn may vary quite a bit depending on where within the sign she was born, as well as a wide range of additional astrological factors. But for now, let's stick to the basics. Just remember: don't jump to conclusions as soon as you meet her. Give her room to shine. Get to know the woman behind the sign.

Her personality: Pros and cons

Pros	Cons
• Persistent	• Snobbish
• Independent	• Stubborn
• Feminine	• Superficial
• Stylish	• A loner
• Passionate	• Pushy
• Neat and organised	• Reserved
• Affectionate	• Cautious
• A perfectionist	• Afraid of showing weakness
• Reliable and loyal	• Afraid of not measuring up
• Intelligent	• Afraid of losing control
• Passionate	• Ruthless
• Ambitious	• Arrogant
• Optimistic	• Self-centred
• Efficient	• Suppresses her feelings

Tip: How to show romantic interest

Old-fashioned attentiveness, generosity and style will always capture her attention. Masculinity is important to her. She is independent and needs a strong man around her.

Romantic Vibes

Miss Capricorn:
The strong and tender partner

The essence

Committed. In her opinion, either you're in a relationship with her or you're not. She knows that a relationship takes commitment, which is why she seldom rushes into things.

Tempted by comfort. Sometimes, she makes choices based on practical preferences rather than her feelings. This can result in short-lived relationships.

Be present, be supportive. Intimacy means a lot to her, and receiving support and encouragement from her man is very important.

Masculinity rules. When it comes to feeling comfortable on an emotional level, she needs a strong and caring man by her side. Although she is independent, she longs for security and protection.

Loyal. When she finally finds the man who satisfies her emotional and practical needs, she will stick with him no matter what happens.

Putting her foot down! Although she is loyal, she is no pushover. She expects the feelings and commitment to be mutual. She may not leave if there's a problem, but she will put her foot down and give her partner a piece of her mind.

Tip: How to show erotic interest

Don't try seducing her if you've only just met her. She needs to feel comfortable around a guy before she beds him. If you do know her, be masculine in your approach. Drop a gentle hint, and use your voice and your eyes to seduce her.

Erotic Vibrations

Miss Capricorn:
The cool and hot lover

The essence

Ease into it. There will be no immediate passion. She takes pride in being cool and controlled.

...or dive in. She will respond quickly to hints and suggestions – provided that she's close to the man and feels comfortable around him. At that point, she will give herself completely and become a passionate partner.

Hot and passionate. She has a strong sex drive and enjoys having sex frequently.

Comfort is a must. In her opinion, sex belongs in the comfort of the bedroom – or at least inside, in a private setting. Don't suggest a quick one in the backseat of your car; you will only be told off.

Don't get kinky. She prefers the traditional and comfortable aspects of sex.

Bring on the main course. As soon as she feels passionate, she will keep going for a long time. Endurance and persistence are her trademark in every aspect of life.

Stamina. She expects her partner to keep it up. A guy who goes to sleep after fifteen minutes of passionate sex will be kicked out of her bed.

CHAPTER 5

COMPATIBILITY QUIZ

Are you banging your head against the wall, or does she unleash your positive potential? Do you provoke her or bring out the best in her? Is she making you throw your arms into the air in exasperation, or do you feel inspired and complete in her company? Take the test to find out.

Question 1
Do you think it's important to be persistent until you have reached your goal?

A. That depends on the goal. Some things are worth fighting for.
B. Of course it's important. How else are you going to succeed?
C. Perhaps, but I'm not that patient.

Question 2.
Do you feel comfortable with traditional sex?

A. It strikes me as quite boring.
B. It's OK, provided I can introduce variations to the old themes every now and then.
C. Yes! Comfortable sex doesn't have to be boring. It can be very passionate.

(cont.)

Question 3.
Do you prefer having sex in unusual places or in private and comfortable surroundings?

A. I prefer sex in comfortable surroundings – and preferably with a bottle of wine.
B. I get a kick out of having sex in unusual places. Traditional routines aren't my thing.
C. I prefer safer and more comfortable surroundings – although I do find the idea of sex on a beach very exciting.

Question 4.
Do you show your romantic feelings?

A. I usually forget, but I'm sure she knows how I feel about her.
B. Reassurance is important for a happy relationship. I regularly tell my girlfriend that I love her.
C. Sometimes I do, sometimes I don't. It depends on the mood.

Question 5.
What kind of woman turns you on?

A. The healthy, outdoorsy type.
B. The playful and girlish type.
C. The stylish, cool and passionate type.

Question 6.
How would you describe yourself?

A. Focused, conservative and serious.
B. Cool, ambitious and wise.
C. Reserved, caring and intelligent.

Question 7.
If you were struggling with a problem, would you tell your partner?

A. Of course. If I can't trust my girlfriend, who can I trust?
B. No, I'm too proud. I prefer to sort things out on my own.
C. I suppose I would tell her, but it depends on what it was about.

Question 8.
Do you think it's possible to express love through sex?

A. I guess ... I don't really think about it.
B. Absolutely! If you cannot express love when you're having sex, you're not on the same level as each other.
C. Sex and love are two different things. Why try to mix them?

Question 9.
You are going away for a week. Would you suggest phone sex?

A. Never – that seems vulgar.
B. Of course! Sex over the phone is good fun.
C. Perhaps, but only if my girlfriend indicated that she'd like to try it.

Question 10.
What kind of foreplay do you prefer?

A. Romantic and sensual, with champagne and soft music.
B. Short and passionate.
C. I'm not too keen on foreplay at all.

SCORE	A	B	C
Question 1	5	10	1
Question 2	1	5	10
Question 3	10	1	5
Question 4	1	10	5
Question 5	5	1	10
Question 6	1	5	10
Question 7	10	5	1
Question 8	5	10	1
Question 9	10	1	5
Question 10	10	5	1

75 – 100

Few worries, if any. Love, affection and passion. Comfort and luxury. This may sound like something from a novel, but when two people who are on the same level manage to find each other, bliss happens. The bond between you will become stronger as time goes by. The support you give each other can provide you with the confidence and enthusiasm you need in order to move onward in your professional lives. A feeling of security makes it feel safe to explore life – together. And your sensual life is just as rewarding. Enjoy!

51 – 74

It seems as though nothing much could possibly go wrong in this relationship. There won't be many arguments – simply because there's not much to argue about. When it comes to sex, you're a rare match. Not many people manage to express love through sex the way you do. Intimacy is a keyword in discussing your relationship. Continue to be the protective man she needs you to be, and the relationship will thrive.

26 – 50

You probably have mixed feelings about this relationship. You respect and admire your partner, but she can be a challenge. She has high expectations, and sometimes you regard them as a little superficial. A nice house and a fancy car aren't everything in life. Maybe you miss the adventure, the unknown and the erotic mysteries – which you never get to explore with her. It's possible that the relationship is moving in a direction that doesn't feel right. Love conquers all – but nothing much happens if you don't communicate and try to solve your differences. The relationship is definitely possible. The question is: Are the two of you interested in pulling together, or will you simply pull apart?

10 – 25

Are things getting a little boring? Nothing new going on in the bedroom? Too much work and no time to play? If the answer is yes, it might be wise to do something about it before the two of you drift apart completely. If the pressure to perform is getting too much to handle, ask her to see you as you are – not as a superhuman. Communication is the first step to understanding each other. Try to approach her in a slightly different way. Give her a little more attention. If the relationship still feels like a hassle, the two of you should consider looking for romance, happiness and sensual fulfilment elsewhere.

Thoughts...
Communication is the key that can open doors. Take time to listen, and listen with an open mind and open heart.

...just a final note:
This book has not been approved by your date and should be treated accordingly. He or she *may* not agree with the content.